This is a work of fiction. Names, characters, places, and incidents are either the product of the author's imagination or are used fictitiously. Any resemblance to actual persons, living or dead, events, or locales is entirely coincidental.

Text and Illustration Copyright © 2022 Carli Valentine
Book design by Carli Valentine

Published in 2022 by Design By Valentine LLC, in North Ogden, UT, USA. All rights reserved. No part of this book may be reproduced or used in any manner without written permission of the copyright owner except for the use of quotations in a book review. For more information, address: carlivalentine@gmail.com

First paperback edition June 2022

Printed and bound in the United States

Library of Congress Control Number: 2022909812

Book authored and illustrated by Carli Valentine

ISBN (Paperback)- 978-1-957505-07-7
ISBN (Hardcover)- 978-1-957505-06-0

Visit www.carlivalentine.com
www.instagram.com/carlivalentineauthor
www.facebook.com/Carli-Valentine-Childrens-Book-AuthorIllustrator-102280112241008/
www.amazon.com/Carli-Valentine/e/B09JL7V5NB/

Dedicated to my dog Penny. May she have an endless supply of cheeseburgers to devour while she romps among the clouds.

Sun STOLE my snowman!

Lightning TOOK my swimming fun.

These THIEVES are all to BLAME.

They **TOOK** the things that I love best.

It made me oh so **MAD!**

All these **FUN THIEVES** wouldn't stop and it made me rather **SAD.**

Sun WARMED my body.

LIGHTNING in a nighttime sky put on a BEAUTIFUL SHOW!

Maybe these FUN THIEVES weren't SO bad after all! Changing the way you look at things can make BIG FRUSTRATIONS SEEM SMALL.

ABOUT THE AUTHOR

Carli Valentine is a children's book author and illustrator. She has authored and illustrated books including Cutest Pumpkin in the Patch, Turkey Trot, Christmas Is A Feeling, Big Plans for Tomorrow and Extra Special Heart. She resides with her husband, Keaton and 2 boys (Finnegan and Lochlan) in Ogden, Utah. When she's not sketching or scribbling down ideas for her children's books she likes to hang out with her family and volunteer at her son's elementary school and dedicates her time to various children's heart defect charities.

MORE BY THE AUTHOR:

Did you enjoy my book?
Don't forget to leave a review!

⭐ ⭐ ⭐ ⭐ ⭐

Made in the USA
Monee, IL
05 December 2024